STANDARD ON AUTOMATED VALUATION MODELS (AVMS)

STANDARD ON AUTOMATED VALUATION MODELS (AVMS)

Revised Approved, July 2018

International Association of Assessing Officers

IAAO assessment standards represent a consensus in the assessing profession and have been adopted by the Board of Directors of the International Association of Assessing Officers (IAAO). The objective of the IAAO standards is to provide a systematic means for assessing officers to improve and standardize the operation of their offices. IAAO standards are advisory in nature and the use of, or compliance with, such standards is voluntary. If any portion of these standards is found to be in conflict with national, state, or provincial laws, such laws shall govern. Ethical and/or professional requirements within the jurisdiction[1] may also take precedence over technical standards.

[1] For example, USPAP, CUSPAP, IVS, EVS.

About IAAO

The International Association of Assessing Officers, formerly the National Association of Assessing Officers, was founded for the purpose of establishing standards for assessment personnel. IAAO is a professional membership organization of government assessment officials and others interested in the administration of the property tax. Over the years IAAO members have developed assessment practice and administration standards and many of these standards have been adopted by state and international oversight agencies, and some have been incorporated into legislation.

IAAO continues at the forefront of assessment in North America and has been expanding its reach to the global community for the last five decades. Because standards form the rules by which North American assessors perform their duties, they may not be directly applicable to an overseas audience. The standards have been updated to also present the broad principles upon which the rules are based. IAAO believes those principles may be adapted to many differing statutory and regulatory scenarios worldwide.

Acknowledgments

The second edition of the AVM Standard (2018) was developed and written through the dedicated efforts of the Technical Standards Committee comprised of Alan S. Dornfest, AAS, Chair Bill Marchand, Doug Warr, August Dettbarn, Wayne Forde, Joshua Myers, and Carol Neihardt. Additionally Patrick M. O'Connor served as a special knowledge expert. The completed document was reviewed and edited by the AVM Standard Review and Edit Special Task Force comprising of August J. Dettbarn, Chair; Peader Thomas Davis; Leandro Escobar; Ingi Finnsson; Randy J. Ripperger, CAE; and Larry J. Clark, CAE.

Revision notes

This standard replaces the 2003 Standard on Automated Valuation Models (AVMs) and is a complete revision.

Published by
International Association of Assessing Officers
314 W 10th St
Kansas City, Missouri 64105-1616
816-701-8100
Fax: 816-701-8149
www.iaao.org
Library of Congress Catalog Card Number: ISBN 978-0-88329-245-7

Produced in the United States of America.

CONTENTS

STANDARD ON AUTOMATED VALUATION MODELS (AVMS)

1. SCOPE

The standard provides principles, guidance, and best practices for developing and using AVMs for the valuation of real property. The standard is organized with each major section beginning with the main principles covered in that section, followed by a description of all principles. Greater detail is found in appendices. Following are the key principles within this section.

Principles

- *Transparency*
- *Public trust — providing confidence for the stakeholders*
- *Broad applicability*
- *Based on statistically sufficient information*
- *Certification and quality assurance*

This standard provides guidance for public and private sector property valuation that depends on Automated Valuation Model (AVM) systems. AVMs can be used when sufficient economic data exists to permit development of representative and valid statistical samples. Models that adhere to the best practices for data verification, data analysis, market analysis, and ongoing quality control present the most reliable value estimates.

The general format of development and use of an AVM described in this standard is shown in *Figure 1.*

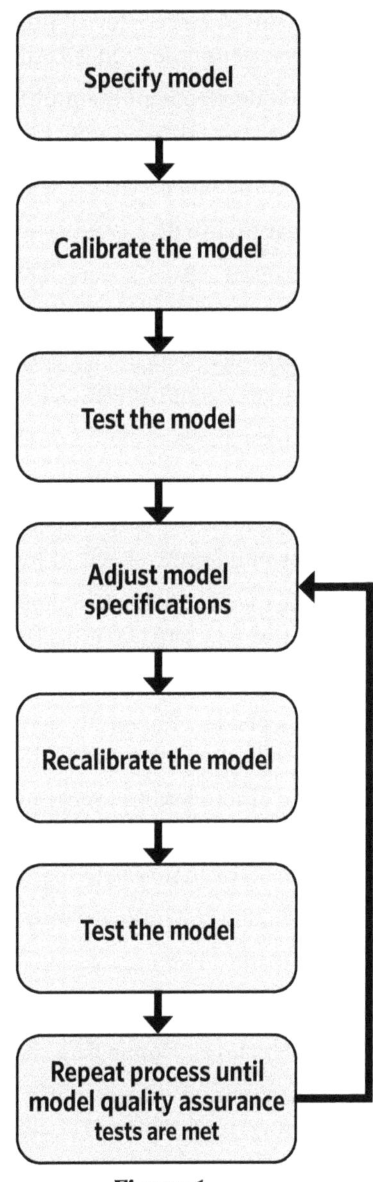

Figure 1

2. PRINCIPLES

- TRANSPARENCY
- Public trust – providing CONFIDENCE for the stakeholders
- Broad APPLICABILITY
- Based on statistically SUFFICIENT information
- Certification and QUALITY ASSURANCE
- Involvement of a QUALIFIED market analyst is highly advisable
- AVM products lead to the development of additional valuation services (APPLICABILITY)
- AVM value estimates developed and operated under this standard may be considered an appraisal (APPLICABILITY)
- Quality assurance for all phases of AVM development and operations is advised (QUALITY ASSURANCE)
- AVM development is a multiple step iterative process (STATISTICAL PRINCIPLES)
- Data availability will influence the model development (SUFFICIENCY)
- Data should be STATISTICALLY verified
- Quantitative data is more objective (STATISTICAL PRINCIPLES)
- Qualitative data is more subjective (STATISTICAL PRINCIPLES)
- Model specification should follow recognized APPRAISAL PRINCIPLES
- Adjustments should be considered for location and market trends (APPRAISAL PRINCIPLES)
- Market analysts should review the data to insure representativeness
- Variable selection requires in-depth knowledge of appraisal and advanced statistical analysis (QUALIFICATION)
- Account for the effects of location (APPRAISAL PRINCIPLES)
- The market analyst should statistically review the reasonableness of the data (STATISTICAL PRINCIPLES)
- Multiple years of market data may be used (STATISTICAL PRINCIPLES)
- Independent appraisals may be used as proxy sales when dealing with limited sales (APPRAISAL PRINCIPLES)
- Use of standardized geographical coordinate systems aids in the capture of location influences (APPRAISAL PRINCIPLES)
- Use of qualitative data requires specialized knowledge (QUALIFICATION)
- Data must be sufficient and representative (SUFFICIENCY)
- Statistical methods should form the basis of quality assurance (QUALITY ASSURANCE)
- Continuous run models require periodic statistical testing
- Sales and economic data should be open market transactions (APPRAISAL PRINCIPLES)
- Both point estimates and reliability measures should be used in evaluating central tendency and variability of results (STATISTICAL PRINCIPLES)
- Samples should be evaluated for outlier influence (STATISTICAL PRINCIPLES)

- Holdout samples or cross validation methods should be used to validate the model's performance (STATISTICAL PRINCIPLES)
- Documentation needs to be available to explain and support the model results (TRANSPARENCY)
- The type of AVM dictates the nature of documentation (PROPORTIONALITY)
- Report design should clearly indicate the value results output by the model (TRANSPARENCY)

3. INTRODUCTION

Principles

- ***Involvement of a qualified market analyst is highly advisable***
- ***AVM products lead to the development of additional valuation services***
- ***AVM value estimates developed and operated under this standard may be considered an appraisal***
- ***Quality assurance for all phases of AVM development and operations is advised***
- ***AVM development is a multiple step iterative process***

3.1 DEFINITION OF AUTOMATED VALUATION MODEL (AVM)

A mathematically based computer software program that market analysts use to produce an estimate of market value based on market analysis of location, market conditions, and real estate characteristics from information that was previously and separately collected. The distinguishing feature of an AVM is that it is a market appraisal produced through mathematical modeling. Credibility of an AVM is dependent on the data used and the skills of the modeler producing the AVM. AVMs should be developed by appropriately qualified market analysts, e.g. appraisers/valuers, who use statistically-based applications to analyze data and select the best simulation of market activity for the analysis of location, market conditions, and property characteristics from previously collected data. AVMs are designed to generate value estimates for properties at specified points in time (retrospective or prospective dates as required by client).

3.2 EXAMPLES OF SPECIFIC AVM PROCEDURES

- AVM Assisting Appraisers [Preliminary Data AVM]
- Appraiser-Assisted AVM [Interactive Valuation Application AVM]
- Repetitive AVM [Continuous Application AVM]
- Blended or Cascading AVM
- Research AVM

AVMs use:

- sales comparison approach;
- cost approach;
- income approach

3.2.1 Preliminary Data AVM [AVM Assisting Appraisers]

After analysts develop the AVM application, appraisers use these AVMs in their professional assignments. Some common uses are:

- Location adjustments
- Time trend adjustments
- Contributory value of building features

The AVM sorts substantial amounts of electronic data and provides selected raw or basic data for interpretation by the appraiser. Appraisers may use the AVM applications to support their opinions of value. These appraisers may provide explanations and use their own data, which they have collected or properly verified.

3.2.2 Interactive Valuation Application AVM [Appraiser-Assisted]

This is a mathematical model application, or a set of applications, that is/are developed, calibrated and checked by analysts with valuation knowledge. In these model applications, an appraiser reviews results and then uses professional judgement to consider modifying model results. Any modification should be subject to quality assurance testing.

3.2.3 Repetitive AVM [Continuous Application AVM]

In this type of AVM, mathematical applications are prepared by an analyst after market analysis. The AVM application is intended to be used repeatedly to project values for future dates, without recalibration but through the addition of new sale prices and economic information. This process may reduce the reliability of the AVM application. If analysts are unsure of the valuation application's ability to generate prospective valuations, the AVM application should be recalibrated.

3.2.4 Blended or Cascading AVM

The cascade process allows application of two or more AVMs using a single interface. The cascade process allows the user to leverage the strengths of multiple AVMs by fitting for location, property type, and projected price range. The weakness of the cascading system is that the user can manipulate the final estimates of value.

3.2.5 Research AVM

Research AVMs are general valuation tools which resemble production AVMs in design, but have limited functionality. Research AVMs are used for initial testing of concepts and are only used for testing purposes. They are used in academic research to measure trends in real estate values. They are also used in public administration such as projecting values for planning or underwriting purposes.

3.3 PURPOSE OF AN AVM

The purpose of an AVM is to efficiently provide an accurate, uniform, equitable estimate of fair market value. Fair market value defined; allowable variance; factors to be considered in determining fair market value; generally accepted appraisal procedures to be utilized. "Fair market value" means the amount in terms of money that a well-informed buyer is justified in paying and a well-informed seller is justified in accepting for property in an open and competitive market, assuming that the parties are acting without undue compulsion. All AVM values should be reviewed for reliability. AVM values generated in compliance with regulations of the governing bodies are considered appraisals. Models that adhere to the best practices for data verification, data analysis, market analysis, and ongoing quality assurance present the most reliable value estimates.

3.4 DEVELOPMENT AND APPLICATION OF AVMS

AVMs are developed using appraisal principles and techniques. Data are acquired and analyzed to develop a market valuation model that can be applied to equivalent properties (sold or unsold) in the same market area. Two major components of valuation modeling are specification and calibration. The model specification process identifies property characteristics (variables) that impact and demand and develops the proposed model structure. Model calibration is the process of deriving coefficients for the variables previously specified in addition variables are created through transformations to avoid collinearity problems. Specification and calibration techniques vary with the purpose of the AVM, type of property, available data, and the experience and knowledge of the market analyst. The basic steps in the development of an AVM are:

- Creation of a scope of work
- Identification and acquisition of property data
- Exploratory data analysis
- Stratification
- Determination of data representativeness
- Model specification
- Model calibration
- Quality assurance
- Model application and value review

Model specification, calibration, and quality assurance are iterative processes that are repeated until statistical diagnostics are satisfactory.

3.4.1 Scope of Work

The scope of work defines the type of property and geographic area in which the AVM will be applied, and the steps required to develop and implement the AVM. The scope of work should state all assumptions, special limiting conditions, and hypothetical conditions.

A key assumption in many AVM applications concerns the current use of the property. Most AVMs implicitly assume the current use is the highest and best use.

3.4.2 Identification and Acquisition of Property Data

Property data needs to be identified and acquired prior to developing an AVM. If the data is not already available, the market analyst should determine what property data is necessary. Property data elements that have a relationship to value may dictate the data collection methods.

Data falls into three broad categories: property data, locational data, and market data. Property data are composed of elements that represent physical attributes of the property. Locational data takes into consideration market demographics, traffic, land use policies, and other geographic factors. Market data include sales, income, and replacement cost information. Data can be acquired from multiple sources:

- Internal resources
- Government sources
- Third party sources
- Public (news) sources
- Client and customer

A primary assumption is that data is reliable when adequate quality assurance is performed through exploratory data analysis. Checks and edits should be made as new data is introduced into the system to ensure compatibility with model specifications.

3.4.3 Exploratory Data Analysis

Data characteristic or attribute analyses include:

- **Data quality review** — completeness and consistency of data, outlier identification and removal
- **Data distributions** — frequency of value-related characteristics
- **Market patterns** — trends in property characteristics, locational analysis using sales data
- **Time trends** — sales frequency and sales dates
- **Discernable patterns and events in the market place** which show effect on buyers and sellers
- **Data element reasonableness**

3.4.4 Stratification

In stratification, properties are organized into homogeneous groups based on factors such as use, physical characteristics, or location. Properties are first stratified by use such as agricultural, apartments, commercial, industrial, or residential. Additional stratification by physical characteristics or value ranges may be performed to minimize the differences within strata and maximize differences among strata. Geographic stratification may be useful wherever the value of various property attributes varies significantly among areas and is particularly effective when housing types and styles are relatively uniform within areas (IAAO 2011, 139–143). However, excessive stratification may provide limited variation in the data. It may be possible to create a global valuation model without stratification, if adjustments for strata attributes (location, use, age, style, etc.) are included as part of the model specification and calibration processes.

3.4.5 Data Representativeness

Data used in developing an AVM model should reflect the subject property or population of properties to produce quality results. The available sales may limit representativeness and applicability of the AVM model. Adequate data means enough sales or economic data with given features for proper adjustments. (See section 6.1)

3.4.6 Model Specification

Model specification is the process of determining the format (mathematical format, such as additive and nonlinear) of the AVM and identifying the variables to be used in the model. (See section 3 and Appendix A)

3.4.7 Model Calibration

Calibration is the process of determining the coefficient associated with each variable, evaluating the significance of the computed coefficients, and examining the coefficients in an AVM to insure they are logical. (See Section 4). Several statistical tools for calibration are found in Appendix B.

3.4.8 Quality Assurance

An AVM should be tested to determine if it meets required accuracy and uniformity standards before initial use and after implementation, depending on risk management policies. This is accomplished through statistical diagnostics and ratio studies in which value estimates are compared to actual values for the same properties. GIS can be used to analyze the spatial trends of the value estimates. Before it is implemented, the AVM also should be tested using sale prices that were not used in the calibration process (e.g., holdout sample or other cross-validation techniques). Properties with unusually large residuals, atypical characteristics, or extreme ratios of model estimates to sale prices, termed "outliers," should be reviewed. Outliers are cases where it is likely that the sale prices (or other value serving as the dependent variable in the model) are not representative, the data are partially incorrect, or the property exhibits atypical features that cannot be adequately accounted for in the model. If the data cannot be corrected, the property should be removed from the sample. (See Section 6)

3.4.9 Model Application and Value Review

Once tested and validated the AVM application can be applied to properties of the same type in the area or region where the model applies. These values should be reviewed for reasonableness and consistency.

4. DATA QUALITY

Principles

- ***Data availability will influence the model development***
- ***Data should be statistically verified***
- ***Quantitative data is more objective***
- ***Qualitative data is more subjective***

Data quality includes evaluation of data availability and accuracy of all physical and market data including property identification and location (e.g., Exploratory Data Analysis).

4.1 DATA AVAILABILITY

The integrity and availability of data will influence the specification of the model and may indicate the need for revisions in the specification and/or limit the usefulness of the resulting value estimates. Attributes used in the model should be examined for quality, completeness and to ensure that attributes are adequately represented. Publicly available data from sources, such as assessors and commercial sector third-party information services are the basis for most AVMs.

When using second and third generation data, it is good practice to verify the accuracy of elements found in the data prior to inclusion in the model. The AVM market analyst should use statistical data analysis to confirm the assumption that the quality of the data will provide reasonable support for the modeling process. The analyst should determine if the data is sufficiently accurate for the intended use.

AVM models are based on a sample of the population. In preparation for model specification the analyst should review the sample data to insure representativeness of the population to which the model will be applied.

4.2 DATA VERIFICATION

Data verification is common in government assessors' AVM development. Market analysts should verify data quality by its relationship to sale prices of properties with similar characteristics. When data items that appraisers would consider highly correlated to value do not prove to have that relationship (based on a correlation matrix or regression t or F values, etc.), this may be an indication of inconsistent data collection or scarcity of data. Data that are inconsistent or with elements missing from the sales file should not be used in the model specification or calibration phases.

4.3 QUALITATIVE AND QUANTITATIVE DATA

Data may be qualitative or quantitative. Quantitative data are objective and can be counted or measured. Ideally, qualitative data are discrete with categorical sublevels. Qualitative data may be descriptive and subjective. Qualitative data such as condition can significantly contribute to the overall value components of land, buildings, and overall general values.

4.4 PROPERTY IDENTIFICATION AND LOCATION

Geographic information systems (GIS) can be used to match AVM system property addresses to addresses in national address files that identify and locate properties by latitude and longitude. For more information on parcel identification see Standard on Digital Cadastral Maps and Parcel Identifiers.

4.5 DATA QUALITY ASSURANCE

Data used in model specification and calibration should pass the following screening tests:

1. Data should be sufficient to produce reasonable valuation models with regard to the property characteristics utilized. In general, the number of sales should be at least five times (fifteen times is desirable) the number of independent variables.
2. Sales used should be valid transactions that reflect market value. Data should be consistent across the population of properties to be valued using the model. Examples include quality, physical condition, and effective age.
3. Property characteristic data should be accurate for use in the model and its application to the population of properties.
4. Sales data and characteristics should be representative of the underlying population or the subset of properties that may be subject to valuation using the AVM.

For transparency, data quality assurance provides a means of evaluating the application of the developed AVM formula to a specific population of properties. The product of that evaluation may include the acceptable ranges of specific property characteristics and ranges of estimated market values to which the model can be applied.

In some circumstances sales used in developing AVM models may not be representative of subject properties for which value estimates are sought. This could be the case, for example, if the model contained few sales with prices or characteristics like those in a high end residential community under development. In this instance, no estimate of value should be provided at those points where the estimates become unreliable due to the data falling outside of acceptable parameters (IAAO Standard on Ratio Studies).

As AVM use increases, new commercial data brokers are emerging to service model developers and operators. These new data warehouses aggregate substantial amounts of data from all available sources, including the use of data scraping. If data scraping is to be used as a data source, it should be done with an understanding of the data format, a quality control plan to keep the data scraping program up-to-date with data formatting changes, and a plan to handle missing data and data in an unexpected form. When employing data scraping consideration must be given to terms of use, data ownership and legal requirements on data use.

5. SPECIFICATION AND CALIBRATION OF AVM MODELS

Principles

- ***Model specification should follow recognized appraisal principles***
- ***Adjustments should be considered for location and market trends***
- ***Market analysts should review the data to insure representativeness***
- ***Variable selection requires in-depth knowledge of appraisal and advanced statistical analysis***

In practice, specification and calibration are performed in an iterative process, which includes the following steps:

1. Specify a model
2. Calibrate the model
3. Test the model
4. Make adjustments to model specification
5. Recalibrate the model
6. Test the model
7. Repeat the process until model quality assurance tests are met

5.1 MODEL SPECIFICATION

AVM models are based upon one or more of the three approaches to value (cost, sales comparison, and income). Model specification starts with review of the data to determine which type of valuation model or models is/are likely to yield the optimal results with respect to the desired quality. Model specification is based on data analysis and appraisal theory. Specification techniques using the three approaches to value are outlined in Appendix A: Model Specification.

5.2 CALIBRATION TECHNIQUES

Model calibration is the development of coefficients through market analysis of the variables in the model. Most AVMs rely on statistics to test the calibration quality. The market analyst may make model specification adjustments via transformations and other techniques until the coefficients are optimized. In addition, coefficient signs should be reasonable and In line with economic theory (i.e.: if there is a statistically significant negative square foot or meter coefficient, the modeler should adjust the specification). Model calibration is part of an iterative process that is repeated until specified statistical diagnostics are met.

The various methods and procedures (some examples are: regression, artificial neural networks) used to calibrate the AVM drive accuracy and credibility of the estimate. Data integrity and the skill level of the analyst contribute to the accuracy of any calibration technique. Users of AVM results should be aware of the interdependence between analyst skills and calibration technologies.

5.3 TIME SERIES ANALYSIS

Time series analyses are techniques that can be used to measure the cyclical movements, random variations, seasonal variations, and cyclical trends observed over time. In property valuation, these analyses can be used to develop a multiplier or index factor to update existing appraised values or to adjust sale prices for individual properties to a valuation date. Since values can change at different rates in different markets, separate factors should be tested for each property type and market area. Specific methods are outlined in Appendix D: Time Series Analysis.

5.4 INDEPENDENT VARIABLE SELECTION FOR MODELS

Modelers should include statistically significant and reasonable variables. Variables (e.g., property characteristics) that are highly correlated with other variables or have a statistically insignificant effect should be excluded or used with caution in the model. Developing a comprehensive criterion for variable selection requires in-depth knowledge in appraisal of various property types, advanced statistical analysis, and mathematics.

5.5 LOCATION

Variables to express the influence of location are critical in any model. The effect of factors external to the property should be determined. To do so, equivalent properties may be grouped by geo-economic area or analyzed at the individual property level. More thorough location analysis should reduce the need for property variables that correlate with location. Methods for analyzing locational influence are explored in Appendix C: Statistical Methods for Developing Location Adjustments.

Geographic stratification is appropriate wherever the value of various property attributes varies significantly among areas and is particularly effective when housing types and styles are relatively uniform within areas. In lieu of geographic stratification, geographic coordinates may be used to account for location. In some populations location stratification and adjustments may not be necessary when model variables already explain most of the difference. (E.g. one location sells for more because it has a lot of homes in "very good" condition. If this is the only reason for the value difference, a variable for "condition" would account for the difference and no further segmentation or locational adjustments would be needed. It also helps make values more defensible

6. MARKET ANALYSIS AND INTENDED USE

Principles

- *Account for the effects of location*
- *The market analyst should statistically review the reasonableness of the data*
- *Multiple years of market data may be used*
- *Independent appraisals may be used as proxy sales when dealing with limited sales*
- *Use of standardized geographical coordinate systems aids in the capture of location influences*
- *Use of qualitative data requires specialized knowledge*

Market analysis steps are similar to those in traditional appraisal, except that more detailed data is used.

Market analysis requires:

- Identification of the property class/type to be valued
- Identification of intended use
- Identification of limited data response
- Identification of the valuation approach(es) to be used
- Identification of property characteristics that have the greatest influence on value
- Identification of geolocational and economic influences

6.1 IDENTIFY THE PROPERTY CLASS/TYPE TO BE VALUED

The AVM requirements to value different property types can vary significantly. An AVM should be optimized to provide accurate estimates of value for specific property types or classes.

6.2 IDENTIFY INTENDED USE

Once the property class or type is determined, the availability of property data and economic information should be used by the analyst to determine the applicability of the estimates of value. Examples of intended use are mortgage loan approval, evaluation of investment portfolios, valuing by assessment jurisdictions, and providing value estimates to the public.

6.3 IDENTIFY LIMITED DATA RESPONSE

Regardless of the property type, when economic or sales information is limited, sales and income data can be expanded by using data from multiple years for similar property types. This may require time trending and related adjustments of sale prices to bring them to current market levels. Independent appraisal of individual unsold properties can also provide comparable data as additional benchmarks.

6.4 IDENTIFY THE VALUATION APPROACH(ES) TO BE USED

The comparable sales, income and cost approaches may be used for all property types based on the data and intended use of the AVM application. Analysts should consider whether land and improvement values are to be presented as separate values from total market value.

When sufficient sales data is available the comparable sales approach is preferred.

When sufficient lease and rental information is available, the income approach may provide the best indicator of market values for income producing properties such as apartments, commercial, industrial and retail properties.

The cost approach provides good indicators of value for specialized properties and properties that have been recently built. The cost approach is also valuable when there is limited sales and/or income information.

Land market analysis may involve only land property characteristics or may be part of improved property market analysis.

AVM developers and analysts should understand the intended use of an AVM before choosing the valuation approach. All recognized valuation approaches may provide indicators of market value.

6.5 IDENTIFY PROPERTY CHARACTERISTICS THAT HAVE THE GREATEST INFLUENCE ON VALUE

The property characteristics that have the greatest influence on value should be identified. Most AVMs use size as the most important variable; land size for land models and building size for improved properties. Other important property characteristics are: age (year built), condition and location. Additional, important characteristics are use of property, type of property, and quality of construction.

Quantitative property characteristics are more reliable and objective. This type of data may be more consistent for use in a model specification. The use of qualitative property characteristics requires additional training and experience because it relies on subjective judgements about the property, therefore the qualitative property characteristics may be more difficult to adapt in model specification.

6.6 IDENTIFY GEOLOCATIONAL AND ECONOMIC INFLUENCES

Geographic coordinate systems may enhance the ability to identify spatial influences. Location analysis relates largely to identifying current use groups of properties subject to similar influences. Economic or outside influences (location) may be dependent on the use of the property. Nuisances for residential properties, such as a railroad track or heavy traffic patterns, could be an important amenity for commercial and industrial properties. It is important that locations adjustments not be based on factors restricted by law or regulation. For example religious orientation.

6.7 CAUTIONS

An analyst may assume that the highest and best use of a property is its current use; however, market analysis may prove otherwise. For example, improved properties (excluding agricultural properties), where the land value is greater than the improvement value, the highest and best use may be subject to change.

Commercial and industrial sales often contain significant amounts of intangible items, which contribute to the reported final settlement price, but are not part of the underlying real property market value. Adjustments during the sales validation process may be required to compensate for the intangible items included in the sale price. Sold properties that include significant amounts of intangible values may be categorized by the analyst as outliers and trimmed.

7. QUALITY ASSURANCE

Principles

- ***Data must be sufficient and representative***
- ***Statistical methods should form the basis of quality assurance***
- ***Continuous run models require periodic statistical testing***
- ***Sales and economic data should be open market transactions***
- ***Both point estimates and reliability measures should be used in evaluating central tendency and variability of results***
- ***Samples should be evaluated for outlier influence***
- ***Holdout samples or cross validation methods should be used to validate the model's performance***

Quality assurance procedures are critical for testing the quality of the data and the applicability of the model.

7.1 MODEL REPRESENTATIVENESS

Samples may become less representative in dynamic markets. In this case, AVM estimates may suffer the effects of time-related errors. When adding sales to an existing model over time, care should be taken to insure the representativeness of the latest sales. During the operational lifetime of the model, periodic quality assurance should be used to capture time related errors.

7.2 MODEL DIAGNOSTICS

The specific diagnostic tools available to market analysts and users of automated valuation models will vary with the model methodology employed. Multiple regression analysis provides the market analyst and user with a wide range of diagnostic statistics that may not be available with other calibration methodologies. In any event, the market analyst must make effective use of the diagnostic tools available during model calibration and be prepared to explain their use and significance to end users.

Standards do not exist for goodness-of-fit statistics (such as the coefficient of determination) or measures of individual variable significance (such as the t-statistic). Nonetheless, the market analyst should be able to explain how those statistics were used and how they relate to the predictive quality of a specific model in relation to the sales data available for calibration.

Various confidence score methods may be found in vendor applications and are referred to in United States federal guidelines (see: Interagency Guidance. 75 Federal Register at 77,469). However, parameters and methodologies for these techniques have not been standardized and it may be difficult to compare similarly named measures produced by different vendor-provided models. This standard takes no position on the validity or usefulness of such guidance.

7.3 RATIO STUDIES

Ratio studies use statistics based on mathematical comparisons between estimated values and sale prices or other dependent variables subject to calibration. The ratios are subjected to statistical analysis to determine central tendency (level), and vertical (value related) and horizontal uniformity or variability. Variability statistics provide information about the degree to which model-determined values are uniform and consistent. While ratio study statistics provide valuable guidance as to the overall quality of the AVM value estimates, statistical measures do not specify the accuracy of individual property estimates.

Sales based ratio studies are among the most objective methods for testing the performance and quality of any valuation system. Because the development and utilization of AVMs are ongoing, without definitive beginning or end dates, sales ratio studies should be performed on a regular, periodic basis to establish the current performance status of the model. Guidance on calculating the statistics recommended in this section is found in the Standard on Ratio Studies. Studies should also be performed on holdout samples to check vertical equity.

7.3.1 Measures of Central Tendency

Measures of central tendency of the ratio of estimated values to sale prices provide an indication of the overall level, with respect to market value. Point estimates of these measures are calculated as shown in table 1, found in Appendix G: Statistical Tables. The median ratio, considered in conjunction with its confidence interval, and distribution of ratios using quantiles and the COD should be used to evaluate whether AVM results attain market value standards.

7.3.2 Measures of Variability

Several statistical tests are available and should be used to determine the degree of variability (uniformity) in the results of any AVM model. Common measures of variability include the coefficient of dispersion (COD) and coefficient of variation (COV). While the COV, based on the standard deviation, is typical in general statistical testing, because of potential for greater distortion of COVs due to outlier inclusion, the COD is recommended as the variability statistic of choice.

7.3.2.1 Coefficient of Dispersion (COD)

In real estate appraisal, the most commonly used measure of variability is the COD, which measures the average absolute percentage deviation of the ratios from the median ratio. The interpretation of the COD does not depend on the assumption that the ratios are normally distributed. Standards for interpreting CODs are contained in the Standard on Ratio Studies.

7.3.2.2 Coefficient of Variation (COV)

The COV is another measure of variability but it may be subject to more outlier effects than the COD. When the ratios are normally distributed the standard deviation and COV enable more specific predictions about the occurrence of various ratios in the population.

7.3.3 Measures of Reliability

An AVM quality assurance statistic calculated from a sample of properties is a point estimate of the corresponding unknown population parameter. A point estimate differs from the unknown value of the population parameter because of sampling error, inherent in every sample. For each measure of AVM quality assurance, the analyst should consider a measure of reliability which explicitly considers such sampling error. Confidence intervals are the most commonly used measure of reliability. A confidence interval is an estimate of the range of values in which an unknown population parameter lies with a given degree of statistical confidence. Confidence intervals can be calculated about any quality assurance measure. For example, if the analyst chooses a 90% confidence level and the sample median sales ratio point estimate from values predicted by the AVM for properties with known sale prices is 95% with a confidence interval lower limit of 88% and upper limit of 102%, then the true median level for the population is between 88% and 102% with 90% confidence. Reliability improves as confidence intervals become narrower, assuming the confidence level remains constant, because the unknown true value for the population parameter falls within a smaller range around the point estimate. However, narrower confidence intervals that result from lower confidence levels may appear to indicate more reliable results, but add uncertainty (i.e. a 70% confidence level will produce a narrower interval than a 90% confidence level, but we have less statistical confidence that the true population parameter is inside the interval).

It is important to form conclusions about AVM quality assurance measures through statistical hypothesis testing because the AVM will ultimately be applied to the population of properties from which the sample was drawn. It is proper to conclude compliance with quality assurance standards unless there are statistical tests that prove, with a high degree of certainty, that standards have not been met. Confidence intervals may be used as such statistical tests and allow conclusions about the unknown population parameter. For example, say the standard is that the level of the value estimate indicated by model results should be within 10% of market value. This standard should be considered met if a 90% two-tailed confidence interval around the median sales ratio overlaps the range of 90% to 110% of market value. Confidence intervals for the applicable measures of appraisal (or AVM value estimate) level are demonstrated in table 1 in Appendix G: Statistical Tables. There are also formulas for developing confidence intervals around the Coefficient of Dispersion (COD) and Coefficient of Price-Related Bias (PRB) (Gloudemans 2011).

7.3.4 Price Related Vertical Inequities

The COD and COV relate to dispersion among the ratios in a stratum, regardless of the value of individual parcels. Another form of dispersion may be systematic differences in the AVM, AVM-assigned values of low-value and high-value properties, termed "vertical" inequity. An index statistic for measuring vertical inequity is the PRD (Price-Related Differential). This statistic should be close to 1.00. Measures above 1.00 tend to suggest regressively while those below 1.00 tend to suggest progressivity. The PRD may not be a reliable measure of vertical inequities, when samples are small, or the weighted mean is heavily influenced by several extreme sale prices. If not representative, extreme sale prices may be excluded from the model prior to the calculation of the PRD. Another measure of vertical inequity is the PRB, which is found by regressing percentage differences from the median ratio on percentage differences in value. The PRB provides a percentage by which model-derived value estimates rise or fall as values double. As a general matter, the PRB coefficient should fall between -0.05 and 0.05. PRBs for which 95% confidence intervals fall outside of this range indicate that one can reasonably conclude that assessment levels change by more than 5% when values are halved or doubled. PRBs for which 95% confidence intervals fall outside the range of – 0.10 to 0.10, indicate very serious vertical inequity. Negative PRBs indicate regressivity while positive PRBs tend to indicate progressivity. See IAAO Standard on Ratio Studies.

7.3.5 Importance of Sample Size

There is a general relationship between statistical precision and the number of observations in a sample drawn from a given population: the larger the sample, the greater the precision and the higher the confidence in the model results. All valid sales should be used unless this results in non-representativeness.

7.3.6 Outliers

Ratios that differ greatly from measures of central tendency may be considered outliers. When the number of outliers is large relative to sample size, the outliers tend to distort ratio study results. Some statistical measures, such as the median ratio, or median percent error are resistant to the influence of outliers. However, the mean and COV, and, to a lesser extent, the COD, are sensitive to extreme ratios. Trimming outliers may be acceptable. See Standard on Ratio Studies for techniques and limitations.

7.4 HOLDOUT SAMPLES

Holdout samples represent groups of valid sales selected in a manner that their characteristics approximate those of the population of properties covered by the automated valuation model. Statistical analysis of such samples can be used to verify results based on the sample of sales used in model development. AVMs can over fit data, and holdout samples are a method to protect against simply choosing the model or models that over fit the most. Inherent in the definition of holdout samples is the premise that the sales not be used in developing the original model. Sales that occur after model calibration can also be used in testing and validating the model. This method may be preferable when few sales are available. Alternatively, cross validation techniques can be used in lieu of traditional holdout samples.

The use of holdout samples to test and verify model-provided value estimates provides an analysis independent from the data used in developing the model. As such, statistical measures of level and variability on value estimates produced by the model, but compared to the holdout sales, would be expected to differ from those directly used in developing the model. The critical issue is the degree of difference in these measures. If there are substantially worse quality assurance statistics in the hold out sample, recalibration of the AVM model may be necessary.

7.5 FREQUENCY OF UPDATES

AVM estimates of value are based on formulas derived from market analysis of a specific geo-economic area during a specified period. Because AVM value estimates are dated, AVM providers should be prepared to update those estimates for significant changes in market conditions and periodically update the underlying models. Movements in the market and the availability of market information should dictate the frequency of this process. Ratio studies and ratio study standards can be used to detect values that drift out of alignment, thereby indicating a need for model updates.

7.6 RECONCILIATION OF VALUES

When a market analysis process involves more than one valuation model, a process of reconciliation is the best practice to adjust to a single final estimate of value. Reconciliation is the process of reviewing the quality/quantity of available data and determining which model to emphasize. Reconciliation includes quality assurance and performance analysis such as ratio studies.

8. DOCUMENTATION AND REPORTS

Principles

- ***Documentation needs to be available to explain and support the model results***
- ***The type of AVM dictates the nature of documentation***
- ***Report design should clearly indicate the value results output by the model***

There should be detailed documentation to support the market analysis process and the final value formula. This documentation should consist of a file that supports the process and methods used to arrive at a final estimate of value and should be available to organize into a report upon request. This report may provide quality assurance statistics.

Some AVM reports are limited to a property identifier and AVM value. Other reports will provide additional information as requested by the clients. AVMs may use additional documentation in separate reports that support the entire AVM model process with individual reports per property that are considered the AVM report.

When more than one value estimate is produced for a subject property, documentation should contain a thorough explanation of the procedures followed to reconcile those candidate estimates into a final estimate of value. Those procedures should include analysis of the relative strengths and weaknesses of each model, and explanation of how that analysis results in a final value estimate.

At a minimum documentation should be comprehensive enough to enable compliance with professional, local, regional or national guidelines and laws. Examples and a list of uses are found in Appendix H: Uses of AVM Reports.

REFERENCES

American Planning Association. 2003. "Land Based Classification Standards." Available from www.planning.org/LBCS/GeneralInfo.

Appraisal Foundation. 2016–2017. *Uniform standards of professional appraisal practice (USPAP).* Washington, D.C.: Appraisal Foundation.

Appraisal Institute. 2015. *The dictionary of real estate appraisal.* 6th ed. Chicago: Appraisal Institute.
Carbone, R. 1976. The design of an automated mass appraisal system using feedback. PhD diss., Carnegie-Mellon University.

Collateral Risk Management Consortium (CRC). 2003. The CRC guide to automated valuation model (AVM) performance testing. Paper presented at Fidelity National Information Solutions (FNIS) Valuation Innovation and Leadership Summit, CRC, May 28, in Laguna Beach, CA.

D'Agostino, R.B., and Stephens, M.A. 1986. *Goodness-of-fit techniques.* New York: Marcel Dekker.

Gloudemans, R. J. 1999. *Mass appraisal of real property.* Chicago: IAAO.

Gloudemans, R., and R. Almy. 2011. *Fundamentals of Mass Appraisal.* Kansas City, MO: IAAO.

Gloudemans, R.J. 2001. Confidence intervals for the coefficient of dispersion: Limitations and solutions. *Assessment Journal* 8 (6):23–27.

Guerin, B.G. 2000. MRA model development using vacant land and improved property in a single valuation model. *Assessment Journal* 7 (4):27–34.

Hoaglin, D.C., Mosteller, F., and Tukey, J.W. 1983. *Understanding robust and exploratory data analysis.* New York: John Wiley & Sons.

United States federal guidelines Interagency Guidance. 75 Federal Register at 77,469).

IAAO. 1990. Property appraisal and assessment administration. Chicago: IAAO.

IAAO. 2013. Glossary for property appraisal and assessment. Chicago: IAAO.

IAAO. 2013. *Standard on ratio studies.* Chicago: IAAO.

Linne, Mark R., Thompson, Michelle. 2010. Visual Valuation: Implementing Valuation Modeling and Geographic Information Solutions. Appraisal Institute.

Mendenhall, W., and Sincich, T. 1996. *A second course in statistics: Regression analysis.* 5th ed. Upper Saddle River, NJ: Prentice Hall.

Tomberlin, N. 1997. "Trimming outlier ratios in small samples." Paper presented at IAAO International Conference on Assessment Administration, September 14–17, at Toronto, ON, Canada.

Waller, B.D. 1999. The impact of AVMs on the appraisal industry. *The Appraisal Journal* 67 (3):287–292.

Ward, R.D., and Steiner, L.C. 1988. A comparison of feedback and multivariate nonlinear regression analysis in computer-assisted mass appraisal. *Property Tax Journal* 7 (1):43–7.

Wollery, A., and Shea, S. 1985. *Introduction to computer assisted valuation.* Boston, MA: Oelgeschlager, Gunn & Hain, Publishers, Inc.

SUGGESTED READING

Abidoye, R.B., and A.P.C. Chan. 2017. "Modeling property values in Nigeria using artificial neural network." *Journal of Property Research* (2017): 1–18.

Bidanset, P.E. 2014. Evaluating spatial model accuracy in mass real estate appraisal: A comparison of Geographically weighted regression and the spatial lag model. *Spatial Analysis and Methods* 16(3): 169–181.

Bidanset, P.E. (2016) "Accurately accounting of AVM land values." Paper presented at IAAO International Conference on Assessment Administration, August 28-31, 2016, at Tampa, Florida.

Birch, J.W., Sunderman, M.A., and T.W. Hamilton. 1991. "Estimating the importance of outliers in appraisal and sales data." *Property Tax Journal* 10.4 (1991): 361–376.

Birch, J.W., Sunderman, M.A. 1996. "Measuring the market movements in assessment districts: Do we need subdistricts," *Assessment Journal* 3(1): 1073–8568.

Bitter, C., Mulilgan, G.F. 2007. Incorporating spatial variation in housing attribute prices: A comparison of geographically weighted regression and the spatial expansion method. *Journal of Geographic Information Systems* 9: 7–27.

Boluwatife Abidoye, R. and A.P.C. Chan. (2016). "Research trend of the application of artificial neural network in property valuation." *International Council for Research and Innovation in Building and Construction.*

Borst, R.A. 2014. *Improving Mass Appraisal Valuation Models Using Spatio-Temporal Methods,* International Property Toronto, Ontario, Canada: Tax Institute.

Boshoff, D., and L. de Kock. 2013. "Investigating the use of Automated Valuation Models (AVMs) in the South African Commercial Property Market." *Acta Structilia.* Bloemfontein, South Africa: University of the Free State.

Bradford, T. and C. Rispin. (2013). Automated valuation models (AVMs). *London, England: Royal Institute of Chartered Surveyors.*

Cannaday, R.E., Sunderman, M.A. 1986. "Estimation of Depreciation for Single Family Appraisals." *Real Estate Economics* 14(2): 175–383.

Colwell, P.F., J.A. Heller, and J.W. Trefzger. 2009. Expert testimony: Regression analysis and other systematic methodologies. *The Appraisal Journal,* Summer 2009, Vol. 77, Issue 3, p253–262.

Chamberlain C, Eckert J K, and O'Connor P M, 1993 "Computer Assisted Real Estate Appraisal: A California Savings and Loan Case Study" *The Appraisal Journal,* October 1993

Chaphalkar, N.B. and S. Sandbhor. (2013). "use of artificial intelligence in real property valuation." *International Journal of Engineering and Technology* 5 (3): 4 p.

d'Amato, M., and T. Kauko, eds. 2017. "Advances in Automated Valuation Modeling: AVM After the Non-Agency Mortgage Crisis." In *Studies in Systems, Decision and Control.* Vol. 86. Edited by J. Kacprzyk, Volume 86. Cham, Switzerland: Springer International Publishing AG.

Demetriou, D. 2016. "GIS-Based Automated Valuation Models (AVMs) for Land Consolidation Schemes." In Proceedings of the 6th International Conference on Cartography and GIS. Eds. T. Bandrova and M. Konecny. Sofia, Bulgaria: Bulgarian Cartographic Association. https://cartography-gis.com/archive-en#archive05 (accessed May 18, 2017).

Donovan, J.D. 2015. "A Framework for Evaluating Automated Valuation Models in Real Estate: an Auditing Perspective." Master's Thesis, Aalto University School of Engineering. https://aaltodoc.aalto.fi/bitstream/handle/123456789/16679/master_Donovan_Jamie_2015.pdf?sequence=1 (accessed May 18, 2017).

Downie, M.L., and G. Robson. 2007. Automated Valuation Models: An International Perspective. Aldwych, London: Council of Mortgage Lenders.

Eckert J K, and O'Connor P M, 1992 "Computer Assisted Review Assurance A California Case Study"

Property Tax Journal, March 1992

Fahrmeir, L., T. Kneib, S. Lang, and B. Marx. 2013. *Regression: models, methods and applications*. New York: Springer Science & Business Media.

Gloudemans 2002. Comparison of three residential regression models: Additive, multiplicative, and nonlinear. *Assessment Journal* 9 (4): .

Gloudemans, R.J. (2004). "AVM quality control". Paper presented at IAAO International Conference on Assessment Administration, August 29-September 1, 2004, at Boston, Massachusetts.

Brunsdon, C., Fotheringham, A. S. and Charlton, M. E. (1996), Geographically Weighted Regression: A Method for Exploring Spatial Nonstationarity. Geographical Analysis, 28: 281–298. doi:10.1111/j.1538-4632.1997.tb00937.xGloudemans, R.J. 2002. Comparison of three residential regression models: Additive, multiplicative, and nonlinear. Assessment Journal 9 (4):25–37.

Kauko, T., and M. d'Amato., eds. 2008. Mass Appraisal Methods: An International Perspective for Property Valuers. Chichester, West Sussex, United Kingdom: Wiley-Blackwell.

Kauko, T., and M. d'Amato. 2004. "Mass Appraisal Valuation Methodologies. Between Orthodoxy and Heresy." In Proceedings of the European Real Estate Society (ERES), No. eres 2004-162.

Linné, M., and M. Thomson. 2010. *Visual Valuation: Implementing Valuation Modeling and Geographic Information Solutions*. Chicago: Appraisal Institute.

Lipscomb, C.A. (2017). "The next generation of AVMs". *Fair & Equitable* 15 (3): 29-33.

Martin, S. (2005). "AVMs in assessment". Paper presented at IAAO International Conference on Assessment Administration, September 18-21, 2004, in Anchorage, Alaska.

McCluskey, W. J. 1997. "Predictive accuracy of machine learning models for mass appraisal of residential property." *New Zealand Valuer's Journal* 16 (4): 41–48.

McCluskey, W., S. Anand. 1999. "The application of intelligent hybrid techniques for the mass appraisal of residential properties," *Journal of Property Investment & Finance*, Vol. 17 (3): 218–239. http://www.emeraldinsight.com/doi/abs/10.1108/14635789910270495 (accessed Oct. 23, 2017). Maloney, J.

Moore, J.W. and J. Myers. 2010. Using Geographic-attribute Weighted Regression for CAMA Modeling, *Journal of Property Tax Assessment & Administration* 7 (3): 5–28.

O'Connor, P.M. 2002. Comparison of three residential regression models: Additive, multiplicative, and nonlinear. *Assessment Journal* 9 (4):37–44.

O'Connor, P.M. 2017. "Residential Valuation Modeling Challenge: Volunteer Modelers Report Their Findings." *Journal of Property Tax Assessment & Administration* 13(2) 69–92.

Peyton, S. 2006 "A spatial analytic approach to examining property tax equity after assessment reform in Indiana" *Journal of Regional Analysis and Policy* 36(2): 182–193.

Maloney J, Ripperger, R., and O'Connor, P.M. 2001. "The first application of modern location adjustments to cost approach and its impact." Linking Our Horizons, Proceedings of the 67th International Conference on Assessment Administration. IAAO, September 9–12, at Miami Beach, FL.

Rossini, P., and P. Kershaw. 2008. "Automated Valuation Model Accuracy: Some Empirical Testing." In Proceedings of the 14th Pacific Rim Real Estate Society Conference. http://prres.net/papers/Rossini_Automated_Valuation_Model_Accuracy_Some_Empirical_Testing.pdf (accessed May 18, 2017).

Sunderman, M. A., and J.W. Birch. "Valuation of land using regression analysis." *Real Estate Valuation Theory* (2002): 325–339.

Sunderman, M.A., Birch, J.W. 2003. "Estimating Price Paths for Residential Real Estate," *Journal of Real Estate Research* 25(3): 277–300.

Tabachnick, B.G., L.S. Fidell, and S.J. Osterlind. 2001. Using Multivariate Statistics, 5th ed . Pearson.

APPENDIX

APPENDIX A. Model Specification

Model specification is the review of the data to determine which valuation models yield the best possible results. Model specification is based on the data analysis and appraisal theory. Model quality is dependent on the experience of the market analysts and the quality of the data. Sample model specifications are provided throughout this appendix.

A.1 COST APPROACH

The cost approach is an indirect method of arriving at market value, based on specification of replacement cost new less depreciation plus market derived land value. The cost approach is calibrated by review of construction costs and sales. This approach generally produces more acceptable results for newer properties, specialized properties and properties with insufficient sales. Model specification for the cost approach requires the estimation of separate land and building values.

Two cost approach formulas for model specification are:

$$MV = \varpi GQ \times [(1 - BQ_D) \times RCN + LV]$$

Where

- *MV* is the market value estimate;
- ϖGQ represents the general qualitative variables such as location, economic adjustments, and time of sale;
- BQ_D is a building qualitative variable representing depreciation;
- *RCN* is the replacement/reproduction cost new;
- *LV* is the land value.

(Gloudemans 1999, 124)

And

$$MV = \varpi GQ \times [(\varpi BQ \times \Sigma BA) + (\varpi LQ \times \Sigma LA) + \Sigma OA]$$

Where

- *MV* is the estimated market value;
- ϖGQ is the product of general qualitative variables;
- ϖBQ is the product of building qualitative variables;
- ΣBA is the sum of building additive variables;
- ϖLQ is the product of land qualitative variables;
- ΣLA is the sum of land additive variables; and
- ΣOA is the sum of other additive variables.

If a third party provides the cost tables, it is the responsibility of the AVM market analyst to calibrate the cost tables to the local market to provide a valid indicator of value by the cost approach. It is also the responsibility of the AVM market analyst to fully understand the assumptions made by the third party in constructing the cost tables, the original source of the construction costs used, and the way the unit-in-place costs were aggregated by the third party to arrive at the published square foot rates.

A.2 SALES COMPARISON APPROACH

The Sales Comparison Approach can be implemented as a comparable sales model or as a direct market model.

A.2.1. Comparable Sales Model

There are two steps in a comparable sales routine. The first step involves the selection of the sales most comparable to the subject propertys, possibly utilizing a dissimilarity measure, such as the Minkowski or Euclidean distance metrics, and a series of data filters. The second step adjusts the sale prices of the comparable sale properties to the subject property based on difference in data characteristics. The adjusted sale prices are then used to determine the estimate of value for the subject property. Both steps in the comparable sales routine may be supported by statistics or a statistically-based direct market model. Model specification for the comparable sales method can be summarized as follows:

$$MV = SP_C + ADJ_C$$

- MV represents the market value estimate;
- SP_C represents the selling price of comparable sale properties; and
- ADJ_C represents adjustments to the comparable sales.

(Gloudemans 1999, 124)

A.2.2 Direct Market Model

An application of the Sales Comparison Approach, using direct market models may take one of three model structures:

- additive (also termed "linear"),
- multiplicative (also termed "log linear"), or
- hybrid (also termed "nonlinear")

A.2.2.1 Additive models

Additive models have the form:

$$MV = B_0 + B_1 \times X_1 + B_2 \times X_2 + \cdots$$

Where

- MV is the dependent variable;
- B_0 is a constant;
- X_1 represents the independent variables in the model; and
- B_1 are corresponding rates or coefficients.

In a direct market model, the dependent variable "MV" is either sale price or sale price per unit.

A.2.2.2 Multiplicative models

In a multiplicative model the variables are either raised to powers or are themselves powers to which coefficients in the model are raised; the results are then multiplied rather than added. An example follows:

$$MV = B_0 \times X_1^{B1} \times X_2^{B2} \times \cdots$$

MV is the dependent variable;

- B_0 is a constant;
- X_1^{B1} where X represents the independent variables in the model; and
- X_1^{B1} where ^{B1} represents the corresponding rates or coefficients.

In this example, each variable is raised to a corresponding power.

Multiplicative models consist of a constant B_0 and percentage adjustments. They have several advantages, including the ability to capture curvilinear relationships more effectively and the ability to adjust proportionately to the value of the property being appraised. Multiplicative models are usually calibrated using linear regression packages. This requires some of the variables to be mathematically transformed for calibration. In this case the market value would require a transformation.

A.2.2.3 Hybrid (Nonlinear) models

Hybrid (nonlinear) models are a combination of additive and multiplicative models. The following example of a hybrid model is specified the same as a cost model and demonstrates the flexibility of the hybrid model.
A hybrid (nonlinear) model specification that separates value into building, land, and "other" components (e.g., outbuildings) is:

$$MV = \varpi GQ \times [(\varpi\ BQ \times \Sigma BA) + (\varpi LQ \times \Sigma LA) + \Sigma OA]$$

Where

- MV is the estimated market value;
- ϖGQ is the product of general qualitative variables;
- ϖBQ is the product of building qualitative variables;
- ΣBA is the sum of building additive variables;
- ϖLQ is the product of land qualitative variables;
- ΣLA is the sum of land additive variables; and
- ΣOA is the sum of other additive variables.

A.3 INCOME APPROACH

The income approach is an indirect method for determining market value. The appraiser evaluates income for quantity, quality, direction, duration, and the expense incurred to earn this income, and then converts it by means of a capitalization rate into an estimate of market value.

In an income model, the dependent variable may be income, income per unit (net rentable area), expenses, and expenses per unit or capitalization rate. The steps in this approach are:

1. Estimate gross income, expenses, and net income from market data.
2. Select the appropriate capitalization method (model specification).
3. Derive a capitalization rate or income multiplier from the market (model calibration).
4. Compute value by capitalization.

While there are many model specifications of the income approach, the basic overall direct capitalization formula is:

$$MV = NOI/R$$

Where

- *MV* is the price examined in the calibration and the resulting estimate of market value;
- *NOI* is the net operating income; and
- *R* is the overall capitalization rate.

Another set of income approach methodologies uses the relationship between gross income and rent. These are commonly known as Gross Income Multipliers (GIM) and Gross Rental Multipliers (GRM).

The model takes the form of:

$$MV = GI_A \times GIM$$

Or

$$MV = GI_M \times GRM$$

Where

- *MV* is the price examined in the calibration and resulting estimate of market value;
- GI_A is the gross annual income;
- *GIM* is the gross income multiplier;

Or

- MV is the price examined in the calibration and resulting estimate of market value;
- GI_M is the gross monthly income;
- GRM is the Gross Rental Multipliers.

APPENDIX B. Calibration Techniques

Model calibration is the development of adjustments or coefficients through market analysis of the variables to be used in an AVM. Many AVMs in use today rely on statistical models as the method of calibration. Some example techniques may be based on regression, geographic-weighted regression, or neural networks. All regression programs are based in statistics, while neural networks draw on the analogies of adaptive biological learning.

B.1 CALIBRATION USING STATISTICALLY BASED METHODS

Multiple regression analysis (MRA) is a statistically based analysis that evaluates the linear and/or curvilinear relationship between a dependent (response) variable and several independent (predictor) variables. Models produced using MRA come with a rich set of diagnostic statistics that provide evaluation tools for the market analyst to compare results between and among specified models. These include "goodness of fit" statistics such as R2, adjusted R2, SEE, COV, and "measures of variable significance", such as R, t, F, etc.

B.1.1 MRA Assumptions

The accuracy and credibility of an MRA model depends on the degree to which certain assumptions are met.

Complete and accurate data are required if MRA is to achieve predictive accuracy. The assumption is that sold properties' data are representative of the properties to which they are applied. Data should also be divided into training samples used to develop the model, and holdout samples (control samples) used to test model results.

MRA requires the assumption of normally distributed errors. Another requirement is that as the price level changes, the error term remains constant or homoscedastic; when unequal variances occur at different price ranges, the error term is heteroscedastic. Multicollinearity describes the condition where independent variables are correlated with each other. A correlation matrix is a valuable tool to test for multicollinearity in which variables are correlated. Undetected multicollinearity may result in use of improper coefficients.

B.1.2 Diagnostic Measures of Goodness-of-Fit

The market analyst should understand how the various key statistical measures relate to the reliability of results. These statistics fall into two categories: overall measures of model performance and individual variable measures that determine how well an individual variable performs. Primary measures of goodness-of-fit for overall model performance are the coefficient of determination (R2), standard error of the estimate (SEE), COV, and average percent error.

Appraisers asked to review AVM results should understand the role that goodness-of-fit statistics play in evaluating AVM results.

B.1.3 MRA Strengths

- Goodness-of-fit statistics – gives credence to the validity of results.
- Software availability – many regression software products are available.
- Wdely accepted calibration method.

B.1.4 MRA Weaknesses

- Requires a level of statistical knowledge – market analysts should possess significant background in data analysis and statistical methods.
- Interactive and nonlinear market trends are difficult to measure without transforming data.

B.2 ARTIFICIAL NEURAL NETWORKS

Another system for calibrating real estate valuation models is Artificial Neural Networks (ANNs). Neural networks can calibrate models that consist of both linear and nonlinear terms simultaneously. The user inputs each variable with assigned weights (coefficients). The software exposes the data using an algorithm in a hidden layer where the weights are adjusted (calibrated) in a manner that reduces the squared error. This is an iterative process much like those found with hybrid (nonlinear) regression. The final output results in a single estimate of value with the exact algorithm remaining hidden from the market analyst.

B.2.1 Strengths of Neural Networks

- The ability of the neural network to "learn" as it goes and to take new information and process it as the network has been trained.
- Neural networks can recognize and match complicated, vague, or incomplete patterns in data.

B.2.2 Weaknesses of Neural Networks

- The complexity of how the process works is in the hidden layer.
- Lack of a definable model structure at the output stage makes explanation of value and support of the value more difficult.
- Lack of goodness-of-fit statistics

B.3 CALIBRATION SUMMARY

The various methods and procedures used to calibrate the AVM are the engines that drive accuracy and credibility of the estimate made. Data quality and the skill level of the analyst are key in defining the accuracy of one calibration technique as compared to others. Users of AVM products should be aware of the interdependence between skills and technologies of calibration when deciding how well the AVM will perform.

This standard encourages AVM market analysts and clients to understand that AVM development is not a black box process; instead, it is based on well-defined concepts surrounding the appraisal process. AVM clients understand that developers of AVM products are not limited to using a single method of calibration. Product market analysts often base their value estimates on multiple technologies.

APPENDIX C. Statistical Methods for Developing Location Adjustments

There are several methods of accounting for location. Two common methods for developing location adjustments are the creation or use of existing geo-economic areas and use of geocoordinates. Geo-economic areas are the traditional and most usual form of location analysis. In AVMs, geo-economic areas may be based upon streets and natural boundaries, and government designated areas.

Geographic coordinate techniques relate common elements such as price to each property's unique location. Software uses a variety of smoothing techniques to compute a unique location adjustment for each property. This variable is then included, along with other variables, in a multiple regression or other model to capture location influences. Geographically Weighted Regression, another method of accounting for location, works by allowing model coefficients to vary by location in order to pick up spatially heterogeneous effects

Model frameworks that incorporate these methods for accounting for location include the following:

- Spatial Regression Model (i.e. Spatial Lag Models, Spatial Error Models);
- Inclusion of Locational Variable in the Model Specification (i.e. - Regression with Locational Binaries, Random Forests with a Locational Variable as a Feature);
- Multi-Stage Locational Adjustment Models (i.e. - Regression Model Paired with Locational Value Response Surface, Market-Adjusted Cost by Geo-economic Area);
- Spatial Interpolation Models (i.e. Kriging);
- Locally-Weighted Regression Model (i.e. - Geographically-Weighted Regression);
- Segmented Models (i.e. - Separate Regression Models by Market Area);
- Cluster Analysis.

APPENDIX D. Time Series Analysis

Time series analyses are techniques that can be used to measure the cyclical movements, random variations, seasonal variations, and trends observed over a period. These analyses can be used to develop a multiplier or index factor to update existing appraised values or to adjust sale prices for individual properties to a valuation date.

Methods used to develop time trend factors for property valuation include:

- Value per-unit analysis;
- Re-sales analysis;
- Sales/assessment or sales/AVM value ratio trend analysis;
- Median/mean value per period in the form of a moving average/median sale price;
- Inclusion of time sale variables in MRA/AVM models.

Value per-unit analyses track changes in sale price per unit (e.g., per square foot for residential properties or per unit for apartments) over time. The method is easily understood and lends itself well to graphical representation, as well as to statistical modeling to extract the average rate of change. A downside is that the method does not account for the myriad of other value influences, such as age and construction quality, that affect per-unit values.
Re-sales analysis uses repeat sales occurring over a given period of time. Price changes between sales are converted to monthly rates and an average (or median) rate of change is extracted. The larger the number of repeat sales, the more reliable the estimated rate of change. The method can overestimate rates of change if repeat sales reflect substantial improvements (or other alterations) made to the property since the first sale. Repeat sales may be too selective and not represent the subject or population of properties to be valued by an AVM.

Sales/assessment (or sales/AVM value) ratio trend analysis involves tracking changes in the ratio of sales prices to existing assessments (or AVM values) made as of a common base date. Increases in the ratios indicate inflation and vice versa. The ratio also provides the index factor required to convert an AVM value to a full value estimate. Like value per-unit analysis, the method lends itself well to graphical and statistical analysis. An advantage of the method is that AVM values account for most value determinants and thus can isolate time trends better than the value per-unit method. The method assumes that the AVM values share a common basis, and its reliability depends partly on the accuracy or uniformity of the AVM values.

Median/mean value per period is taught in many of the courses offered to single property appraisal specialists and real estate sales personnel as a quick method to arrive at a time adjustment to allow the use of older sales in special cases. The modeler collects all sale prices from a region for a specific type of property under study. The sales are grouped into periods of one or three months and a simple average or median price per period is calculated. The average or median prices per period are regressed to establish a trend line. The trend value is then used to adjust the sale price to the effective date of the valuation. This has become popular with spreadsheet valuation models used for market analysis and price opinions found on local real estate sites. The method has the same limitation as value per-unit analysis, in that it does not account for the myriad of other factors that affect sales prices.

Once a time trend is established, it can be used to adjust values to any point within the sales period. Trend factors can be extrapolated for a brief period beyond the sales period, but this should be done with caution and grows increasingly unreliable as the period is lengthened.

APPENDIX E. Modeling For AVMs

When adequate sales data are available, the sales comparison approach is the preferred method of valuing all property. The approach may take two forms: direct market models and comparable sales. When adequate sales data are not available, cost or income approach models may apply.

Direct market models developed from sales analyses use various model structures, with coefficients derived via a mathematical calibration method. The comparable sales method is a two-part method in which comparable sales are found and then adjusted to the subject property. Whether automated or appraiser derived, all market analysis relies on the quality and experience real estate appraisers/valuers.

E.1 MARKET SALE BASED MODELS

E.1.1 Comparable Sales Models

Comparable sales models use sale prices of properties with attributes similar to the subject property to establish estimates of market value. It essentially requires two models. The first one is a comparable selection model. The advantage of this model is that all recent sales with proximity to the subject are considered. When the comparable sales have significant attribute differences, the confidence of the adjustments begins to suffer. For selecting quality comparable sales, an AVM analyst may consider a routine that uses a weighted selection model (e.g., regression coefficients, Minkowski or Euclidian distance metrics). Once the best comparable sales are selected, they should be adjusted for attributes that are dissimilar to the subject. Comparable sales models that are supported by direct market models that use quantitative methods to derive the adjustments are more stable, reliable and statistically supported than simple matched pairs analysis.

In its formatted form, the comparable sales approach should display how each attribute adjustment in the AVM contributes to the overall value estimate. Users of AVMs are cautioned that matched pairs analysis is not a statistical calibration method.

E.1.2 Direct Market Models

The basic premise of direct market models is that the price of a marketed good is related to its characteristics or the services it provides. Direct market models lend themselves well to the calibration methods and techniques discussed throughout this standard. Properly designed direct market models will produce AVMs capable of accurate and credible value estimates.

- Additive models sum the variables multiplied by their coefficients.
- In multiplicative models, variables are raised to powers or are themselves powers to which coefficients are raised. Results are multiplied together. These models may better provide for curvilinear functions.
- Hybrid (nonlinear) models provide the most flexibility because they accommodate monetary and percentage adjustments. In addition, non-linear hybrid models can produce separate land and building values. These models may better provide for curvilinear functions.

E.2 INCOME MODELS

The income approach can be used to develop AVMs for all leased properties (land and/or buildings), because most types of income producing property may be sold based on their income streams. The two most commonly used approaches are direct capitalization and gross income multipliers (GIM). Discounted cash flow (DCF) analysis may also be used. Assumptions for DCF analysis, including anticipated yield, holding period, and value at the end of that period, can be difficult to derive from the market.

E.2.1 Modeling Gross Income

Gross incomes may be obtained from local market surveys or industry publications. Gross income models are easier to develop than net income models because the data is easier to obtain and less subject to manipulation. Gross income models can be developed for either potential or effective gross incomes.

E.2.2 Vacancy and Collection Losses from Potential Gross Income (PGI)

Vacancy and collection losses are deducted from the PGI to account for typical losses due to vacancy and bad debts based on local market conditions. The vacancy and collection losses usually vary by property use and are expressed as a percentage of the annual PGI. The percentage may be determined by a market analysis of PGIs compared with actual income through market analysis, or from information supplied by local lenders, government assessors and industry trade publications.

E.2.3 Modeling Expenses

Expense data may be obtained from the same sources as revenue data. Expense ratios can be developed by either stratification or a modeling approach. Where insufficient data are available for multiple models, a single expense ratio model may be developed by determining a reference use or occupancy group.

E.2.4 Direct Capitalization

Direct capitalization involves developing an overall rate (OAR) directly from the market. The OAR is then used with the estimated net income to estimate the value by income capitalization. Like expense ratios, capitalization rates can be developed using either stratification or a modeling approach. The direct capitalization rate is the estimated net income divided by the sale price.

E.2.5 Gross Income Multiplier (GIM)

GIM models involve developing coefficients directly from the market place for either the potential gross income or the effective gross income, depending on the data collected. Effective Gross Income Multiplier models are generally more stable. GIMs have the advantage of not requiring expense data. It is important to ensure that variables related to differences in expense ratios are included because gross incomes are unadjusted for expenses.

E.2.6 Property Taxes

In income models care should be taken to treat property taxes consistently in the development and application of AVMs. Property taxes may be included as an expense or as a component of the OAR.

E.3 COST APPROACH BASED MODELS

E.3.1 Cost Models

The cost approach works best when applied to specialized properties or properties that do not exhibit a great deal of measurable depreciation, and where the land value can be reasonably estimated from recent land sales. Replacement cost models are anchored in tables developed by studying local building cost data. Many replacement cost new tables (RCN) are calibrated with sales of newly built properties. These RCN estimates need further calibration for actual property condition (depreciation), location (macro and micro), and a supportable estimate of vacant land value, to arrive at estimates of market value.

E.4 LOCATION VALUATION ADJUSTMENT

Two methods of accounting for location are the delineation of geo-economic areas and the use of GIS parcel coordinates. Geo-economic areas can be used as categorical variable in a model specification. Separate models can be developed by geo-economic area or areas. GIS parcel coordinates provide options for modeling, such as locational value response surface analysis (LVRSA) or geographically weighted regression (GWR). Methods of accounting for location are found in Appendix C.

When using geo-economic area approaches, boundaries may be drawn to coincide with major streets, natural barriers, and/or political subdivision boundaries. The market analyst should be aware that location adjustments can change abruptly from one submarket and boundaries may change over time.

GIS may be used as an aid in delineating geo-economic areas. GIS may be used to display an existing response surface or to calculate a response surface as the variance in value on a three-dimensional plane. Where a GIS is not available, geoeconomic areas can be developed based on appraisal judgment, or grids can be developed and x, y coordinates manually derived from the grids.

E.5 DEVELOPMENT OF THE LAND MODEL(S)

Sales comparison is the primary approach for estimating the market value of land. The valuation of land by sales comparison shares many of the same analyses and modeling processes with improved valuation models.

For leased land, and agricultural and rural properties, where insufficient sales are available, a capitalized income stream is commonly used to estimate the market value. Income land appraisal relies on capitalized income analysis.
Land values may be modeled separately from improved values, or vacant and improved property may be modeled in a single combined valuation model (Guerin 2000). The primary benefit of a combined model is that both vacant and improved sales are used, which significantly increases the sales sample size for analysis and modeling. When developing a combined model, a binary variable should be used to separate vacant and improved sales. In addition, separate time and size adjustments should be tested for vacant and improved sales.

Income data can be used to value rented or leased land. Income capitalization for land follows the same general principles as commercial and industrial properties.

APPENDIX F: Value Justification

Market analysts should be prepared to review and justify values developed through AVMs. The review process includes:

- finding evidence that data sources are accurate and consistently collected
- implementation of stratification testing
- preparation of a listing of comparable sales
- preparation of a list of listing prices
- performance of ratio studies on comparable sales as well as hold out samples
- evaluating the consistency of values or sales prices of similar properties within the locational area
- preparation of documentation

It may be possible to support value estimates derived from one AVM with estimates derived from alternative methods. The fact that a property sold for a price different from the AVM estimate does not mean that the AVM estimate is wrong. AVM estimates represent market value and price is an historical fact. Begins with checking the statistical accuracy of the data in the sample used to develop the AVM. It is strongly recommended that a stratification testing methodology be implemented. For example, stratification may be by neighborhood or age.

There should be documentation to allow clients and other intended users to understand in nontechnical terms how the model was developed and applied.

If the user modifies the AVM produced values, they assume complete responsibility for the results and the effects on the quality assurance measures. In this instance, original quality assurance measures may not be applicable.

APPENDIX G: Statistical Tables

TABLE 1. Example of Ratio Study Statistical Analysis Data Analyzed

Rank of ratio of observation	Appraised Value (AV in $)	Market Value (MV in $)	Ratio (AV/MV)
1	48,000	138,000	0.348
2	28,800	59,250	0.486
3	78,400	157,500	0.498
4	39,840	74,400	0.535
5	68,160	114,900	0.593
6	94,400	159,000	0.594
7	67,200	111,900	0.601
8	56,960	93,000	0.612
9	87,200	138,720	0.629
10	38,240	59,700	0.641
11	96,320	146,400	0.658
12	67,680	99,000	0.684
13	32,960	47,400	0.695
14	50,560	70,500	0.717
15	61,360	78,000	0.787
16	47,360	60,000	0.789
17	58,080	69,000	0.842
18	47,040	55,500	0.848
19	136,000	154,500	0.880
20	103,200	109,500	0.942
21	59,040	60,000	0.984
22	168,000	168,000	1.000
23	128,000	124,500	1.028
24	132,000	127,500	1.035
25	160,000	150,000	1.067
26	160,000	141,000	1.135
27	200,000	171,900	1.163
28	184,000	157,500	1.168
29	160,000	129,600	1.235
30	157,200	126,000	1.248
31	99,200	77,700	1.277
32	200,000	153,000	1.307
33	64,000	48,750	1.313
34	192,000	144,000	1.333
35	190,400	141,000	1.350
36	65,440	48,000	1.363

TABLE 1.1. Results of statistical analysis

Statistic	Result calculated on preceding data
Number of observations in sample	36
Total appraised value	$3,627,040
Total market value	$3,964,620
Average appraised value	$100,751
Average market value	$110,128
Mean ratio	0.900
Median ratio	0.864
Weighted mean ratio	0.915
Price-related differential (PRD)	0.98
Price-related bias (PRB) coefficient (t-value)	0.233 (3.02)
PRB 95% two-tailed confidence interval	(0.081 - 0.384)
Coefficient of dispersion (COD)	29.8%
Standard deviation	0.297
Coefficient of variation (COV)	33.0%
Probability that population mean ratio is between 90% and 110%	49.7%
95% mean two-tailed confidence interval	0.799-1.000
95% median two-tailed confidence interval	0.684-1.067
95% weighted mean two-tailed confidence interval	0.806-1.024
Shape of distribution of ratios	Normal (based on binomial distribution)
Date of analysis	9/99/9999
Category or class being analyzed	Residential

TABLE 2. Ratio Study Performance Standards

Type of property — General	Type of property — Specific	COD Range**
Single-family residential (including residential condominiums)	Newer or more homogeneous areas	5.0 to 10.0
Single-family residential	Older or more heterogeneous areas	5.0 to 15.0
Other residential	Rural, seasonal, recreational, manufactured housing, 2-4-unit family housing	5.0 to 20.0
Income-producing properties	Larger areas represented by large samples	5.0 to 15.0
Income-producing properties	Smaller areas represented by smaller samples	5.0 to 20.0
Vacant land		5.0 to 25.0
Other real and personal property		Varies with local conditions

These types of property are provided for guidance only and may not represent jurisdictional requirements.

Appraisal level for each type of property shown should be between 0.90 and 1.10, unless stricter local standards are required.

PRD's for each type of property should be between 0.98 and 1.03 to demonstrate vertical equity.

PRD standards are not absolute and may be less meaningful when samples are small or when wide variation in prices exist. In such cases, statistical tests of vertical equity hypotheses should be substituted (see table 1-2).

Alternatively, assessing officials can rely on the PRB, which is less sensitive to atypical prices and ratios. PRB coefficients should generally fall between −.05 and .05. PRBs that are statistically significant and less than −0.10 or greater than 0.10 indicate significant vertical inequities.

*** CODs lower than 5.0 may indicate sales chasing or non-representative samples. (See Standard on Ratio Studies)*

APPENDIX H: Uses of AVM Reports

AVM reports may have many uses. This standard will only list some of the typical uses.

H.1 REAL ESTATE LENDERS

- Reduce time to approve real estate loan applications;
- Provide unbiased estimate of value for loan underwriting;
- Provide real estate value/scores to compliment borrower's credit scoring;
- Standard estimates for annual review of individual appraiser's performance;
- Quality assurance for selling pooled loans;
- Review of loan portfolios;
- Support for lending decisions and geographic distribution required by the Community Reinvestment Act;
- Statistical support for litigation;
- Updates current valuation of portfolio properties;
- Support in purchase of loan portfolios or lending institutions;
- Portfolio valuation reviews by secondary mortgage markets and bond rating firms;
- Systematic review of mortgage loan transaction to assist in the discovery of potential systematic fraud.

H.2 REAL ESTATE PROFESSIONALS

- Support in setting listing price;
- Support in negotiation between sellers and buyers;
- Central database for appraisers;
- Selection of appropriate economic information to support subject property;
- Support for appraiser's opinions of value;
- Support for appraiser's review and desktop appraisal assignments;
- Support for appraisal consulting assignments that involve large numbers of properties;
- Statistical support for litigation.

H.3 GOVERNMENT

- Planning and land use decisions;
- Development of value estimates for review by assessment staff appraisers;
- Standardized estimates of value to annually review field appraisers' performances;
- Valuation substitutes for appraisals in ratio study reports;
- Screening of sale prices for valid market sales transactions;
- Audits of lenders by state and federal regulators;
- Assist states with standardized values to review property assessments in school funding formulas;
- Fraud identification and prevention by enforcement, taxation, customs, and oversight agencies (such as GSE, HUD, IRS, Canada Mortgage and Housing Corporation, Statistics Canada, and state and national bank regulators);
- Fraud prosecution by comparing transactions to standardized values;
- Assist in valuation for right-of-way and property condemnation cases;
- Support for prior values in disaster situations to provide efficiencies is economic rebound of communities.

H.4 GENERAL PUBLIC

- Support for various business development and economic decisions;
- Assistance in determining best listing price;
- Assistance in determining best offering price;
- Review of local government tax assessments;
- Estate estimates of real estate value by attorneys and estate administrators.

H.5 AD VALOREM TAX

- Estimating mass appraisal values;
- Support of values in appeals and litigation;
- Appraisal quality control;
- Study of the effects on valuation of contaminated properties;
- Studies used in the analysis of fiscal planning.

AVM reports may be sufficient as stand-alone products, or they may lead to a request for a more detailed appraisal report based on the needs and usage of the intended user. This listing is only a portion of the potential uses of AVMs. When clients request AVMs for a limited and specific use, the AVM report will provide quality information to the intended user quickly and inexpensively.

APPENDIX I: Use of AVM Reports as A Complete Single Property Appraisal Report

I.1 CREDENTIALING OF AVM DEVELOPERS AND END USERS

Appraisal reports used for the determination of collateral value, Ad valorem value or in meeting reporting requirements of regulated businesses and individuals often require value certification by a person holding formal credentials as an appraiser or valuer. One method of meeting this need is in the model developer and supervising end user holding credentials from a recognized organization in the development and use of mass valuation methods. Additionally the community of end users of AVM output should receive training in basic AVM theory and the strengths and weaknesses of AVM based valuation.

I.2 REPORTING FORMAT FOR FINIANCIAL AND AD VALOREM USES

Appraisal/valuation reports used for the determination of collateral value, Ad valorem value or regulated filing and reporting often require special reporting formats. Often these reports require presentation of the data used and the methods employed in the value estimate. The developer should be made aware of these requirements as an aid to insure required transparency.

GLOSSARY

Algorithm – Computer-oriented, precisely defined set of steps that, if followed exactly, will produce a prespecified result (for example, the solution to a problem).
Additive Model – A model in which the dependent variable is estimated by multiplying each independent variable by its coefficient and adding each product to the constant.

Automated Valuation Model – A mathematically based computer software program that market analysts use to produce an estimate of market value based on market analysis of location, market conditions, and real estate characteristics from information that was previously and separately collected. The distinguishing feature of an AVM is that it is a market appraisal produced through mathematical modeling. Credibility of an AVM is dependent on the data used and the skills of the modeler producing the AVM.

Backwards Regression – A form of stepwise regression starting with all candidate variables entering the model, then removing and testing the effect of each deletion of each variable using a chosen model fit criterion, deleting the variable (if any) whose loss gives the most statistically insignificant deterioration of the model fit, and repeating this process until no further variables can be deleted without a statistically significant loss of fit.

Binary (Dummy) Variable – (1) Binary variables are qualitative data items that have only two possibilities – yes or no (for example, corner location). (2) A variable for which only two values are possible, such as results from a yes-or-no question; for example, does this building have any fireplaces? Used in some models to separate the influence of categorical variables. Also called an indicator variable, dichotomous variable, or dummy variable.

Blended or Cascading AVM – An AVM that produces two or more value estimates that are reduced to a final value estimate through reconciliation.

Cluster Analysis – A statistical technique for grouping cases (for example, properties) based on specified variables such as size, age, and construction quality. The objective of cluster analysis is to generate groupings that are internally homogeneous and highly different from one another.

Coefficient – In a mathematical expression, a number or letter preceding and multiplying another quantity.

Comparable Sales Model – The model selects "similar sales" using some standard criteria. It then rates those comparable sales by suitability, based on the physical and sales characteristics of each comparable sale, by adjusting the varying elements (much as is done on an appraisal form); the model then calculates an estimate of value.

Confidence Interval – The range of values, calculated from the sample observations, which are believed, with a particular degree of confidence, to contain the true population parameter (mean, median, COD, etc.) The confidence interval is not a measure of precision for the sample statistic of point estimate, but a measure of the precision of the sampling process.

Confidence Score – The AVM Confidence Score is a value that indicates the level to which each of multiple AVM models "agrees" with the other estimated values for a given property.

Constrained Variable – A variable limited to a defined range of values in order to force a coefficient to take a defined value, it is used in multivariable linear regression to aid in explanation of the model. Land value is often constrained to the value used in the cost approach to avoid the discussion of land have one value in cost and another in market.

Cost Approach – One of the three approaches to value, the cost approach is based on the principle of substitution–that a rational, informed purchaser would pay no more for a property than the cost of building an acceptable substitute with like utility. The cost approach seeks to determine the replacement cost new of an improvement minus depreciation plus land value.

Cross Validation – A technique for validating an AVM where, iteratively, a subset of sales is held out of the model and the model is re-fit to the remaining sales. The analyst could then examine either the predictive results for the subsets of holdout sales or the model coefficients over the various iterations.

Data Scraping – A technique using software programs that can analyze human-readable data, typically unstructured, from websites and store it in a structured data file. Collection methods included text filtering, analysis and, capture and image analysis and optical character recognition.

Direct Capitalization – The conversion of expected income and rate of return into an estimated present value when using the income approach to determine value.

Direct Market Method/Analysis – One of two formats of the sales comparison approach to value (the other being the Comparable Sales Method). In the direct market method, the market analyst specifies and calibrates a model used to estimate market value directly using multiple regression analysis or another statistical algorithm.

Euclidean Distance Metric – A measure of straight-line distance between two points. In property valuation, it is used to find the nearest neighbor or similar property based on an index of dissimilarity between property location and attributes. When using multivariate selection, the squared difference is divided by the standard deviation of the variable to normalize the differences. (Also see Minkowski Distance Metric.)

Forward Regression – A form of stepwise regression which involves starting with no variables in the model, the model is tested with the addition of each variable using a chosen model fit criterion, adding the variable (if any) whose inclusion gives the most statistically significant improvement of the fit, and repeating this process until the addition of new variables improves the model to a statistically significant extent.

Geographic Information System (GIS) – (1) A database management system used to store, retrieve, manipulate, analyze, and display spatial information. (2) One type of computerized mapping system capable of integrating spatial data (land information) and attribute data among different layers on a base map.

Geoeconomic Area – (1) The environment of a subject property that has a direct and immediate effect on value. (2) A geographic area (in which there are typically fewer than several thousand properties) defined for some useful purpose, such as to ensure for later multiple regression modeling that the properties are homogeneous and share important locational characteristics.

Geoeconomic Area Analysis – A study of the relevant forces that influence property values within the boundaries of a homogeneous area.

Goodness-of-Fit – A statistical estimate of the amount and hence the importance, of errors or residuals for all the predicted and actual values of a variable. In regression analysis, for example, goodness-of-fit indicates how much of the variation between independent variables (property characteristics) and the dependent variable (sales prices) is explained by the independent variables chosen for the AVM.

Heteroscedasticity – Nonconstant variance in error terms and model residuals; specifically, in regression analysis, a tendency for the errors to increase (fan out) as the dependent variable increases.

Hit Rates – The number of times the model or cascading models return a useable value estimate. Not a measure of how well the models fit the data but a measure of the relative success of a model in providing a useable result. Systems with high hit rates often result in a lower cost per valuation because of wider area of property they may be used on.

Holdout Sample – Part of a set of data set aside for testing the results of analysis.

Homogeneous – Possessing the quality of being alike in nature and therefore comparable with respect to the parts or elements; said of data if two or more sets of data seem drawn from the same population; also said of data if the data are of the same type (that is, if counts, ranks, and measures are not all mixed together).

Income Approach – One of the three approaches to value, based on the concept that current value is the present worth of future benefits to be derived through income production by an asset over the remainder of its economic life. The income approach uses capitalization to convert the anticipated benefits of the ownership of property into an estimate of present value.

Interactive Valuation Application AVM [Appraiser-Assisted] – This is a mathematical model application, or a set of applications, that is/are developed, calibrated and checked by analysts. This provides estimates of value that are reviewed and used by valuer.

Location Value Response Surface Analysis (LVRSA) – A mass appraisal technique that accounts for location as a variable that is defined by a three dimensional surface.

Location Variable – A variable that seeks to measure the contribution of locational factors to the total property value, such as the distance to the nearest commercial district or the traffic count on an adjoining street.

Market – (1) The topical area of common interest in which buyers and sellers interact. (2) The collective body of buyers and sellers for a product.

Market Analysis – A study of real estate market conditions for a specific type of property.

Market Analyst – An analyst who studies real estate market conditions and develops mathematical algorithms that represent those market conditions.

Market Area – An area defined on the basis that the properties within its boundaries are more or less equally subject to a set of one or more economic forces that largely determine the value of the properties in question.

Market Value – Market value is the major focus of most real property appraisal assignments. Both economic and legal definitions of market value have been developed and refined. A current economic definition agreed upon by agencies that regulate federal financial institutions in the United States is:

The most probable price (in terms of money) which a property should bring in a competitive and open market under all conditions requisite to a fair sale, the buyer and seller each acting prudently and knowledgeably, and assuming the price is not affected by undue stimulus. Implicit in this definition is the consummation of a sale as of a specified date and the passing title from seller to buyer under conditions whereby:

- The buyer and seller are typically motivated;
- Both parties are well informed or well advised, and acting in what they consider their best interests;
- A reasonable time is allowed for exposure in the open market;
- Payment is made in terms of currency or in terms of financial arrangements comparable thereto.

The price represents the normal consideration for the property sold unaffected by special or creative financing or sales concessions granted by anyone associated with the sale.

Mean – A measure of central tendency. The result of adding all the values of a variable and dividing by the number of values.

Median – A measure of central tendency. The value of the middle item of an uneven number of items arranged or arrayed according to size; the arithmetic average of the two central items in an even number of items similarly arranged.

Minkowski Distance Metric – The Minkowski Metric measures the distance between a subject property and potential comparable properties based on the sum of the absolute value of the differences. (See Euclidean Distance Metric)

Model – (1) A representation of how something works. (2) For purposes of appraisal, a representation (in words or an equation) that explains the relationship between value or estimated sale price and variables representing factors of supply and demand.

Model Calibration – The development of the adjustments or coefficients from market analysis of the variables to be used in an automated valuation model.

Model Deployment – the application of a finalized model to data (existing or new), typically in a platform outside of the statistical package used to specify, calibrate, and develop the model.

Model Specification – The formal choosing of a model methodology (e.g., multiple regression analysis, geographically weighted regression, multiplicative, or hybrid) and subsequent development in a statement or equation, based on data analysis and appraisal theory.

Multicollinearity – Correlation among two or more variables. In regression analysis, high multicollinearity among the independent variables complicates modeling and will compromise the reliability of the resulting coefficients. If the multicollinearity is perfect, the multiple regression algorithms simply will not work and either an error message may result, or the software may purge one or more of the problem variables.

Multiple Regression Analysis (MRA) – A statistical technique, similar to correlation, used to analyze data in order to predict the value of one variable (the dependent variable), such as market value, from the known values of other variables (called "independent variables"), such as lot size, number of rooms, and so on. If only one independent variable is used, the procedure is called simple regression analysis and differs from correlation analysis only in that correlation measures the strength of the relationship, whereas regression predicts the value of one variable from the value of the other. When two or more variables are used, the procedure is called multiple r egression analysis.

Multiplicative Model – A mathematical model in which the coefficients of independent variables serve as powers (exponents) to which the independent variables are raised, or in which independent variables themselves serve as exponents; the results of which are then multiplied to estimate the value of the dependent variable.

Neural Network – An artificial neural network (ANN) is a collection of mathematical models that emulate some of the observed properties of biological nervous systems and draw on the analogies of adaptive biological learning. An artificial neural network has several key elements: input, processing (calibration), and output. Other names associated with neural networks include connectionism, parallel distributed processing, neuro-computing, natural intelligent systems, and machine learning algorithms.

Nonlinear Model – Model that incorporates both additive and multiplicative components. (See also Additive Model, and Multiplicative Model.)

Outlier – An observation that has unusual values, that is, it differs markedly from a measure of central tendency. Some outliers occur naturally; others are due to data errors.

Preliminary Data AVM [AVM Assisting Appraisers] – This AVM sorts substantial amounts of electronic data and provides selected raw or basic data for interpretation by the appraiser. The appraisers use the AVM applications to provide their opinions of value.

Ratio Study – In the context of AVM output, a study of the relationship between model-produced values and market values. Of common interest in ratio studies are the level and uniformity of the ratios.

Research AVM – general valuation tools which resemble production AVMs in design, but have limited functionality. Research AVMs are used for initial testing of concepts. They are finding application in value projection for public financing.

Repetitive AVM [Continuous Application AVM] – This AVM application is intended to be used repeatedly to project values for future dates, without recalibration but through the addition of new sale prices and economic information.

Sales Comparison – One of the three approaches to value, the sales comparison approach estimates a property's value (or some other characteristic, such as its depreciation) by reference to the sales of similar/comparable properties.

Stepwise Regression – A kind of multiple regression analysis in which the independent variables enter the model, and leave it, if appropriate, one by one according to their ability to improve the equation's power to predict the value of the dependent variable.

Stratification — The division of a sample of observations into two or more subsets according to some criterion or set of criteria. Such a division may be made to analyze disparate property types, locations, or characteristics, for example.

Time Series Analysis — A family of techniques that can be used to measure the cyclical movements, random variations, seasonal variations, and secular trends observed over a period.

Variable — An item of observation that can assume various values, such as square feet, sales prices, or sales ratios. Variables are commonly described using measures of central tendency and dispersion.

Weighted Mean — An average in which each value is adjusted by a factor reflecting its relative importance in the whole, before the values are summed and divided by their number.

www.ingramcontent.com/pod-product-compliance
Ingram Content Group UK Ltd.
Pitfield, Milton Keynes, MK11 3LW, UK
UKHW051129260726
13967UKWH00010B/2941

9 780883 292457